DISCOVER 🐾 DOGS WITH
THE AMERICAN CANINE ASSOCIATION

I LIKE

HUSKIES!

Linda Bozzo

It is the Mission of the American Canine Association (ACA) to provide registered dog owners with the educational support needed for raising, training, showing, and breeding the healthiest pets expected by responsible pet owners throughout the world. Through our activities and services, we encourage and support the dog world in order to promote best-known husbandry standards as well as to ensure that the voice and needs of our customers are quickly and properly addressed.

Our continued support, commitment, and direction are guided by our customers, including veterinary, legal, and legislative advisors. ACA aims to provide the most efficient, cooperative, and courteous service to our customers and strives to set the standard for education and problem solving for all who depend on our services.

For more information, please visit www.acacanines.com, e-mail customerservice@acadogs.com, phone 1-800-651-8332, or write to the American Canine Association at PO Box 121107, Clermont, FL 34712.

Published in 2017 by Enslow Publishing, LLC.
101 W. 23rd Street, Suite 240, New York, NY 10011

Library of Congress Cataloging-in-Publication Data
Names: Bozzo, Linda.
Title: I like huskies! / Linda Bozzo.
Description: New York, NY : Enslow Publishing, 2017. | Series: Discover dogs with the American Canine Association | Includes bibliographical references and index. | Audience: Ages 5 and up. | Audience: Grades K to 3.
Identifiers: LCCN 2015044843| ISBN 9780766077843 (library bound) | ISBN 9780766077973 (pbk.) | ISBN 9780766077652 (6-pack)
Subjects: LCSH: Siberian husky--Juvenile literature.
Classification: LCC SF429.S65 B697 2016 | DDC 636.73--dc23
LC record available at http://lccn.loc.gov/2015044843

Printed in Malaysia.

To Our Readers: We have done our best to make sure all website addresses in this book were active and appropriate when we went to press. However, the author and the publisher have no control over and assume no liability for the material available on those websites or on any websites they may link to. Any comments or suggestions can be sent by e-mail to customerservice@enslow.com.

Photo Credits: Cover, p. 1 ARTSILENSE/Shutterstock.com; p. 3 iStock.com/Katerina_Brusnika; p. 4 Hramovnick/Thinkstock; p. 5 Voltgroup/Shutterstock.com; p. 6 MilicaStankovic/Thinkstock; p. 7 Alexey Savchuk/Shutterstock.com; p. 9 ADRIAN DENNIS/AFP/Getty Images; p. 10 iStock.com/Rythor Breuyeu; p. 11 Morgancapasso/Thinkstock; p. 13 iStock.com/cynoclub; p. 13 jclegg/Shutterstock.com (collar), Aleksey Stemmer/Shutterstock.com (bed), Pattakorn Uttarasak/Shutterstock.com (brush), PERLA BERANT WILDER/Shutterstock.com (dish); Napat/Shutterstock.com (leash), cynoclub (toys); p. 14 Apple Tree House/Thinkstock; p. 15 Tannis Toohey/Toronto Star/Getty Images; p. 16 JOE KLAMAR/ AFP/Getty Images; p. 17 castenoid/Shutterstock.com; p. 18 iStock.com/Vadimguzhva; p. 19 iStock.com/Susan Chiang; p. 21 iStock.com/-10PHOTO-; p. 22 Arnaldo Magnai/Getty Images Entertainment/Getty Images.

E ‖ **Enslow Publishing**
101 W. 23rd Street
Suite 240
New York, NY 10011
USA
enslow.com

CONTENTS

IS A HUSKY RIGHT FOR YOU?

Well-trained and exercised huskies make great family pets. If you do not have other small pets, a husky might be right for you.

Huskies are known for being sled dogs in snowy climates. They have no shortage of energy.

Huskies are not the best choice for first-time dog owners.

A DOG OR A PUPPY?

Huskies do not train well. Good, firm training is a must for this puppy. If you do not have time to train a puppy, an older husky may be better for your family.

Huskies grow to be medium in size, 45–60 pounds (20–27 kilograms).

LOVING YOUR HUSKY

Loving your husky will not be hard to do. Pet him. Read to him. Walk him. Keep your husky busy.

EXERCISE

Huskies enjoy long walks on a **leash**. They need lots of exercise. Play games, like **fetch**, with your husky so he will not get bored.

Huskies will run away. Never let your husky off his leash unless in a fenced-in area.

FEEDING YOUR HUSKY

For their size, huskies do not need a large amount of food.

Dogs can be fed wet or dry dog food. Ask a **veterinarian** (vet), a doctor for animals, which food is best for your dog and how much to feed her.

Give your husky fresh, clean water every day.

Remember to keep your dog's food and water dishes clean. Dirty dishes can make a dog sick.

Do not feed your dog people food.
It can make her sick.

Your new dog will need:

a collar with a tag

a bed

a brush

food and water dishes

a leash

toys

GROOMING

Huskies **shed** more than some other breeds. This means their hair fails out. Brushing your husky will help keep him clean and looking his best.

Use a gentle soap made just for dogs.

Your dog will need a bath every so often. A husky's nails need to be clipped. A vet or **groomer** can show you how. Your dog's ears should be cleaned, and his teeth should be brushed by an adult.

WHAT YOU SHOULD KNOW

Huskies need high fences to keep them from escaping the yard.

Huskies get bored easily. They can get into trouble if left alone too long.

Huskies enjoy howling but rarely bark.

Huskies are hunters. They should be kept away from small animals both indoors and outside.

Huskies are known as escape artists. They will jump, dig, and chew their way out of almost anything.

You will need to take your new dog to the vet for a checkup. He will need shots, called vaccinations, and yearly checkups to keep him healthy. If you think your dog may be sick, call your vet.

A GOOD FRIEND

Huskies can live up to 15 years. You will have lots of time to enjoy this fun-loving dog. Huskies are good friends to everybody.

Huskies don't make good watchdogs because they are so friendly and rarely bark.

NOTE TO PARENTS

It is important to consider having your dog spayed or neutered when the dog is young. Spaying and neutering are operations that prevent unwanted puppies and can help improve the overall health of your dog.

It is also a good idea to microchip your dog, in case he or she gets lost. A vet will implant a painless microchip under the skin, which can then be scanned at a vet's office or animal shelter to look up your information on a national database.

Some towns require licenses for dogs, so be sure to check with your town clerk.

For more information, speak with a vet.

There are many dogs, young and old, waiting to be adopted from animal shelters and rescue groups.

Words to Know

fetch – To go after a toy and bring it back.

groomer – A person who bathes and brushes dogs.

leash – A chain or strap that attaches to the dog's collar.

shed – When dog hair falls out so new hair can grow.

vaccinations – Shots that dogs need to stay healthy.

veterinarian (vet) – A doctor for animals.

Balto was a famous Husky that led a dog sled team that delivered medicine to sick children in Alaska in 1925.

Read About
Dogs

Books

Johnson, Jinny. *Siberian Husky*. Mankato, MN: Smart
Apple Media, 2013.

Markovics, Joyce L. *Sled Dogs*. New York, NY: Bearport
Publishing, 2014.

Websites

American Canine Association Inc., Kids Corner
acakids.com/

National Geographic for Kids, Pet Central
kids.nationalgeographic.com/explore/pet-central/

PBS Kids, Dog Games
pbskids.org/games/dog/

INDEX

A
activity level of huskies, 4
animal shelters, 20, 21

B
bathing, 15
beds for dogs, 13
brushing, 13, 15

C
collars for dogs, 13

D
dishes for dogs, 12, 13

E
exercise, 4, 11

F
feeding, 12, 13

G
games for dogs, 11
grooming, 15

H
hunters, huskies as, 16

I
items needed for dogs, 13

L
leashes, 11, 13
licenses for dogs, 20
lifespan of huskies, 19

M
microchips, 20

N
nail clipping, 15

O
other pets and huskies, 4

P
personality of huskies, 4, 16
puppies, 7, 11

R
running away and huskies, 11, 16, 17

S
size of huskies, 7, 12
sled dogs, 4
spaying/neutering, 20

T
tags for dogs, 13
toys for dogs, 13
training, 4, 7

V
vaccinations, 18
veterinarians, 12, 15, 18, 20

W
walks, 8, 11
watchdogs, 19
water, 12, 13